D1265777

Superstars
of the
GREEN BAY
PACKERS

by M. J. Cosson

amicus
high interest

Amicus High Interest is published by Amicus
P.O. Box 1329, Mankato, MN 56002
www.amicuspublishing.us

Library of Congress Cataloging-in-Publication Data
Cosson, M. J.
  Superstars of the Green Bay Packers / M. J. Cosson.
     pages cm. -- (Pro sports superstars)
  ISBN 978-1-60753-525-6 (hardcover) -- ISBN 978-1-60753-555-3 (eBook)
  1. Green Bay Packers (Football team)--History--Juvenile literature. 2.
Football players--United States--Biography--Juvenile literature. I. Title.
  GV956.G7C67 2014
  796.332'640977561--dc23
                              2013006855

Photo Credits: Greg Trott/AP Images, cover; Morry Gash/AP Images, 2,
15; David Stluka/AP Images, 5, 20; John Lindsay/AP Images, 7; AP Images,
8, 11; NFL Photos/AP Images, 12; Charles Krupa/AP Images, 16, 22; Kevin
Terrell/AP Images, 19, 22

Produced for Amicus by The Peterson Publishing Company
and Red Line Editorial.

Editor Jenna Gleisner
Designer Becky Daum
Printed in the United States of America
Mankato, MN
July, 2013
PA 1938
10 9 8 7 6 5 4 3 2 1

TABLE OF CONTENTS

MEET THE GREEN BAY PACKERS

The Green Bay Packers have won 13 championships. That is more than any other **NFL** team. They have won four Super Bowls. The Packers have had many stars. Here are some of the best.

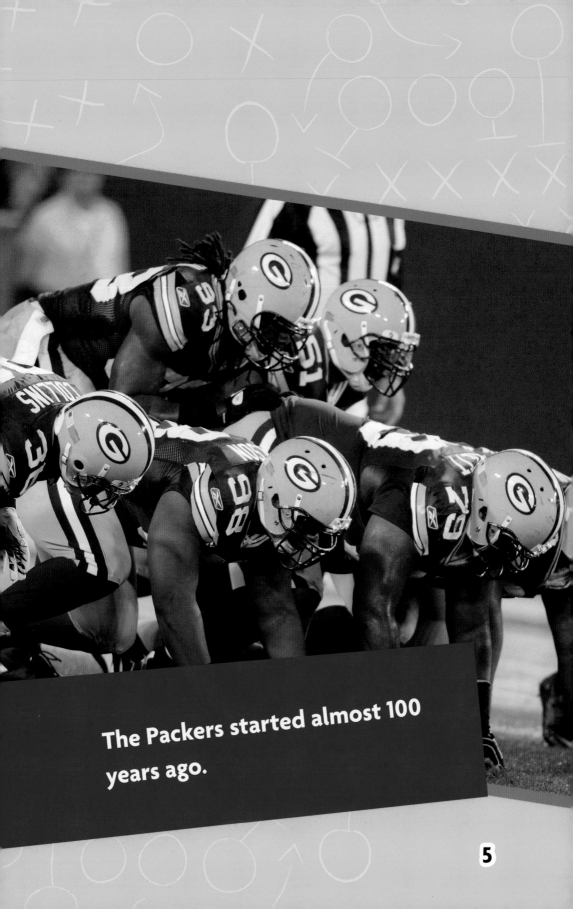

The Packers started almost 100 years ago.

DON HUTSON

Don Hutson was great at catching. He helped change the game of football. Teams mostly ran the ball back in the 1930s. Hutson was one of the first great pass-catchers. He set records that still stand today.

BART STARR

Bart Starr led the Packers' **offense**. He was a smart **quarterback**. He was a great passer. He helped the Packers win the first two Super Bowls.

Starr was the Super Bowl MVP in 1967 and 1968.

PAUL HORNUNG

Paul Hornung was a great football player. Some called him the Golden Boy. He could kick. He could run. He could pass. He could score touchdowns. He was part of the 1960s All-Decade Team.

RAY NITSCHKE

Ray Nitschke played **defense**. He made six tackles in the very first Super Bowl. That was in 1967. He made nine tackles in the second Super Bowl.

BRETT FAVRE

Brett Favre had a strong arm. He was a great quarterback. He joined the Packers in 1992. He played for them for 16 years. He helped take the team to two Super Bowls.

Favre holds many NFL records.

REGGIE WHITE

Reggie White was one of the best defensive players. He was tough. He hardly ever missed a game. White made many **sacks**. He helped the Packers win the Super Bowl in 1997.

White played in 13 Pro Bowls.

AARON RODGERS

Aaron Rodgers plays offense. He is a great passer. He has a strong arm. He has set many records for passing. He was MVP of the 2011 Super Bowl.

CLAY MATTHEWS

Clay Matthews is a **linebacker**. He is good at making sacks. He is not just big. He is quick, too. He helped the Packers win the 2011 Super Bowl.

The Packers have had many great stars. Who will be the next star?

TEAM FAST FACTS

Founded: 1919

Nicknames: Green and Gold, The Pack; fans are called Cheeseheads

Home Stadium: Lambeau Field (Green Bay, Wisconsin)

Super Bowl Titles: 4 (1966, 1967, 1996, and 2010)

NFL Championships: 1929, 1930, 1931, 1936, 1939, 1944, 1961, 1962, and 1965

Hall of Fame Players: 22, including Don Hutson, Bart Starr, Paul Hornung, Ray Nitschke, and Reggie White

WORDS TO KNOW

defense – the group of players that tries to stop the other team from scoring

linebacker – a player whose main job is to tackle the ball carrier so he cannot score

MVP – Most Valuable Player; an honor given to the best player each season

NFL – National Football League; the league pro football players play in

offense – the group of players that tries to score

Pro Bowl – the NFL's all-star game

quarterback – a player whose main jobs are to lead the offense and throw passes

sack – a tackle of the quarterback on a passing play

LEARN MORE

Books

Green, David. *101 Reasons to Love the Packers*. New York: Stewart, Tabori & Chang, 2012.

LeBoutillier, Nate. *The Story of the Green Bay Packers*. Mankato, MN: Creative Education, 2008.

Web Sites

Green Bay Packers Official Site
http://www.packers.com
Watch video clips and view photos of the Green Bay Packers.

NFL.com
http://nfl.com
Check out pictures and your favorite football players' stats.

NFL Rush
http://www.nflrush.com
Play games and learn how to be a part of NFL PLAY 60.

INDEX